J B Machad
Gagne, Tammy
Day by day with Manny
    Machado

$18.50
ocn847537467
06/16/2014

RANDY'S
CORNER

DAY BY DAY WITH...

MANNY MACHADO

BY
TAMMY GAGNE

Mitchell Lane
PUBLISHERS

P.O. Box 196
Hockessin, Delaware 19707
Visit us on the web: www.mitchelllane.com
Comments? Email us:
mitchelllane@mitchelllane.com

Printing   1   2   3   4   5   6   7   8   9

RANDY'S CORNER

DAY BY DAY WITH. . .

Alex Morgan	Manny Machado
Beyoncé	Mia Hamm
Bindi Sue Irwin	Miley Cyrus
Chloë Moretz	Missy Franklin
Dwayne "The Rock" Johnson	Selena Gomez
Eli Manning	Shaun White
Gabby Douglas	Steve Hillenburg
Justin Bieber	Taylor Swift
LeBron James	Willow Smith

Library of Congress Cataloging-in-Publication Data
Gagne, Tammy.
 Day by day with Manny Machado / by Tammy Gagne.
    pages cm. — (Randy's corner)
 Includes bibliographical references and index.
 ISBN 978-1-61228-454-5 (library bound)
1. Machado, Manny, 1992—Juvenile literature. 2. Baseball players—United States—Biography—Juvenile literature. I. Title.
 GV865.M213G34 2014
 796.357092—dc23
 [B]
                                                                          2013023046
eBook ISBN: 9781612285139

ABOUT THE AUTHOR: Tammy Gagne has written dozens of books for children, including *Buster Posey* and *Mike Trout* for Mitchell Lane Publishers. A native New Englander, her heart belongs to the Boston Red Sox. Through her writing, though, she has become a fan of many talented players from other major league teams as well.

PUBLISHER'S NOTE: The following story has been thoroughly researched and to the best of our knowledge represents a true story. While every possible effort has been made to ensure accuracy, the publisher will not assume liability for damages caused by inaccuracies in the data and makes no warranty on the accuracy of the information contained herein. This story has not been authorized or endorsed by Manny Machado.

In 2010, the Baltimore Orioles chose high school shortstop Manny Machado as the third overall draft pick. They offered him a $5.25 million signing bonus to join their team. It was the second-largest bonus in the team's history.

Born on July 6, 1992, in Miami Florida, Manny was only 18 years old when he joined the Orioles. But he already had an impressive record in the sport of baseball. He had a batting average of .639 with 12 home runs and 68 RBIs in 29 games for Brito Miami Private School in Florida.

MANNY AT BRITO

Manny started playing baseball when he was just six years old. He always played the position of shortstop. The Orioles' scouting director, Joe Jordan, told *The Baltimore Sun* that Manny had everything that a scout looks for in a shortstop. "And we feel like he is going to be able to contribute to a game every night in some way."

MANNY DURING HIS LITTLE LEAGUE YEARS

For two years Manny played shortstop for different Orioles minor league teams. On August 8, 2012, though, the team called him up to the majors.

Manny told *The Baltimore Sun* he was shocked when he heard the news. "I didn't know what to say. I was tingling everywhere."

The first thing Manny did when he found out that he was getting moved up to the majors was call his mother, Rosa Nunez, who raised him as a single mother. She was so surprised that she thought he was joking.

ORIOLE PARK AT CAMDEN YARDS

His second call was to his uncle, Geovany Brito, who had taught Manny about the game of baseball when he was a kid. Geovany cried when he heard his nephew's big news.

Manny would be playing third base for the Orioles. He was nervous about this big change. He had only played third base three times in his entire life: once when he was just 13 years old, and twice when he was playing in the minors.

Manny decided to turn to one of his role models for advice. He sent a text to Alex Rodriguez of the New York Yankees.

Manny and A-Rod had a lot in common. They were both born in the US to Dominican parents and grew up bilingual in single-parent households in Miami. Both had been drafted while still in high school. The two even wear the same number on their jerseys: 13. A-Rod assured Manny that everything would work out.

A-ROD'S JERSEY

RODRIGUEZ 13

Manny didn't waste his amazing opportunity with the Orioles. His second time at bat, he hit a triple. "Oh man, it was a load off my shoulder," Manny told *The Baltimore Sun*. "I got my first hit, it was a triple, and I'm just happy to get a hit." He kept the ball as a reminder of his opening day in the major leagues.

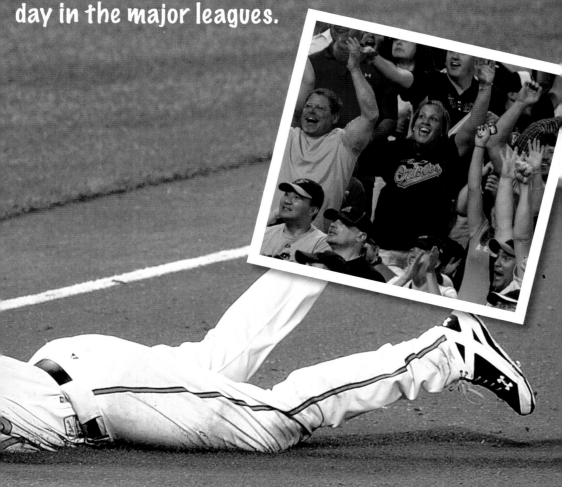

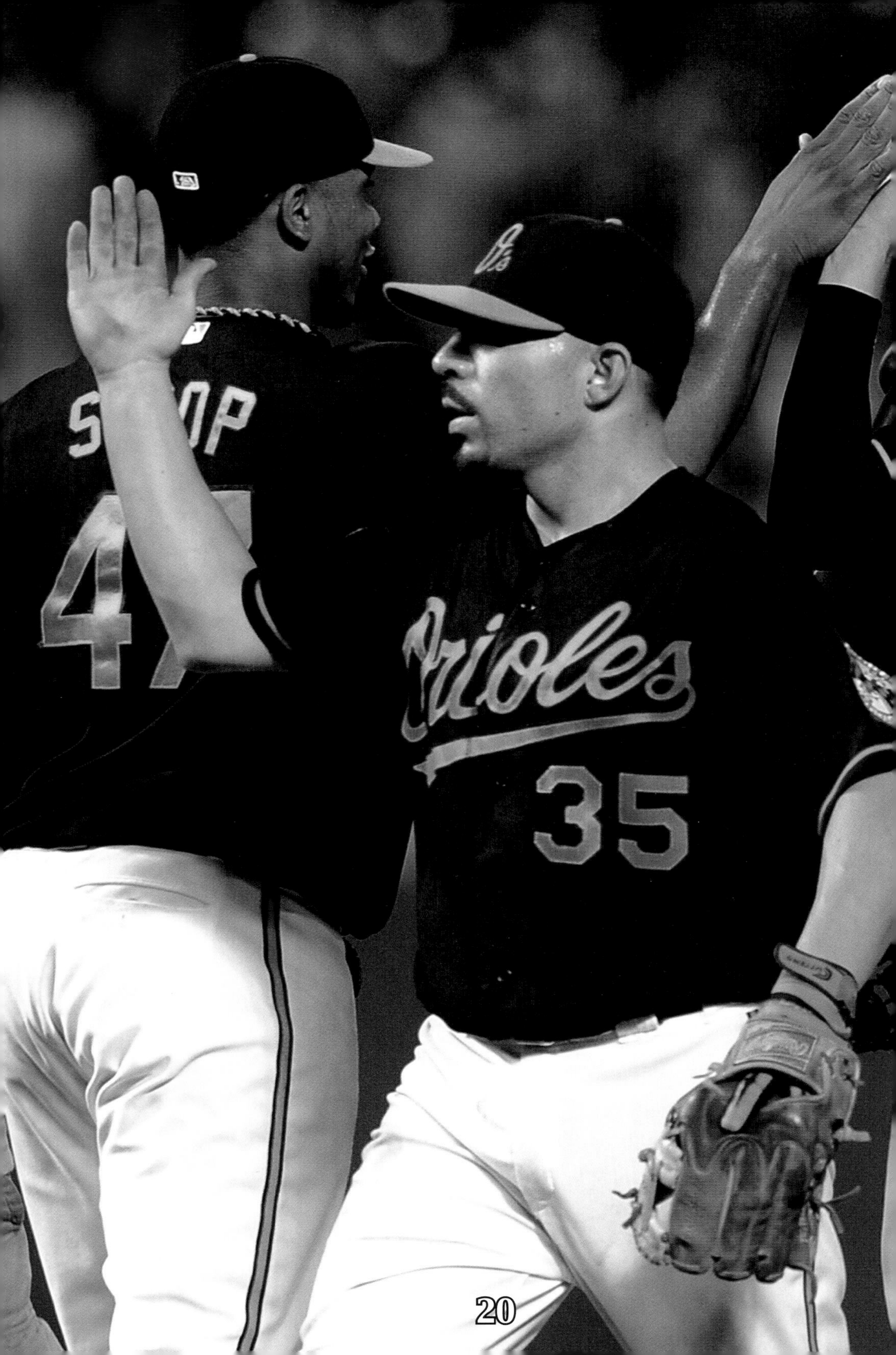
Orioles
35

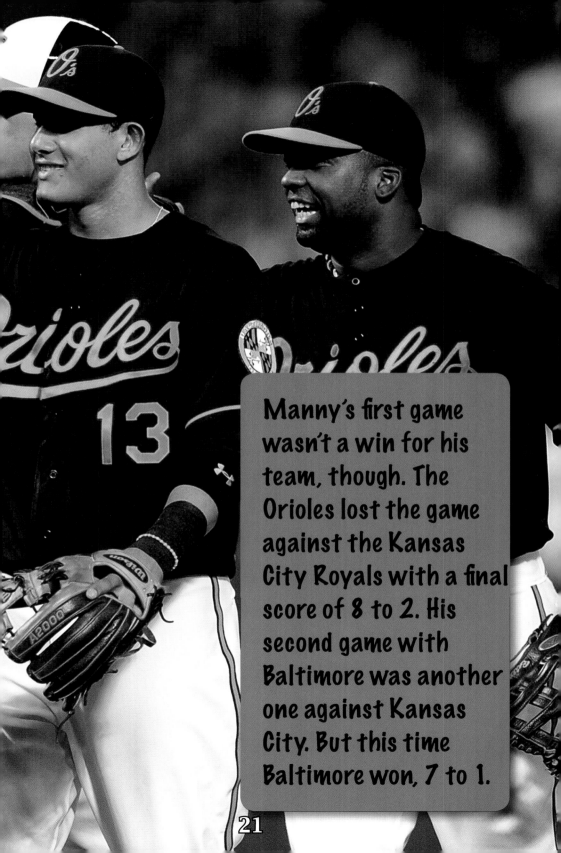

Manny's first game wasn't a win for his team, though. The Orioles lost the game against the Kansas City Royals with a final score of 8 to 2. His second game with Baltimore was another one against Kansas City. But this time Baltimore won, 7 to 1.

In Manny's second game with the Orioles, he also earned a spot in the team's record books. He hit two home runs during the game. Manny was now the youngest Orioles player ever to hit more than one home run in a single game. He was exactly 20 years and 35 days old at the time.

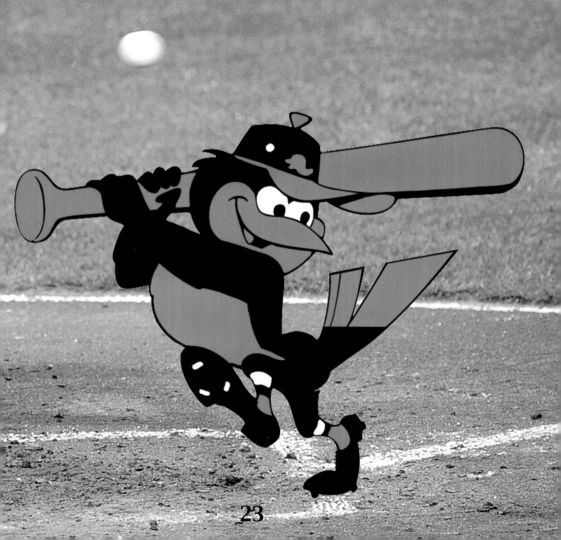

As soon as Manny hit his second homer, the enormous crowd began to cheer. They chanted, "Man-ny, Man-ny!" Orioles outfielder Adam Jones pushed Manny up to the top step of the team's dugout so the crowd could see their new hero. "I've dreamed about that my whole life," Manny admitted to *The Baltimore Sun*, "about going out there and getting that curtain call and [in my] second game in the big leagues I get it."

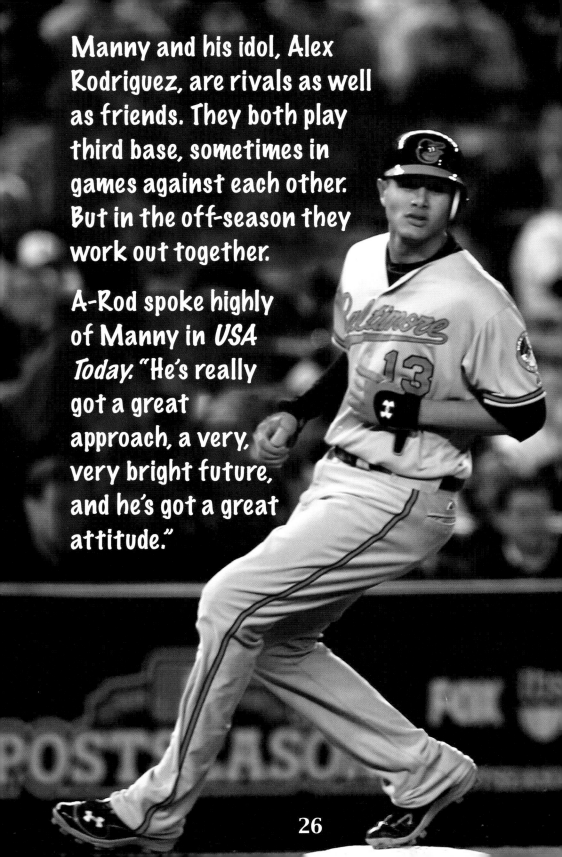

Manny and his idol, Alex Rodriguez, are rivals as well as friends. They both play third base, sometimes in games against each other. But in the off-season they work out together.

A-Rod spoke highly of Manny in *USA Today.* "He's really got a great approach, a very, very bright future, and he's got a great attitude."

ALEX
RODRIGUEZ

"What he's been able to do at 20 years old makes me very proud of him."

ADAM JONES

Manny told *The Baltimore Sun* that teammate Adam Jones gave him some advice early on. After Manny's first hit, Jones told him, "Now that you've got that over with, now it's time to play ball. Now it's time to come up here and do what you're told to do and what you were brought up here to do."

MANNY'S BOBBLEHEAD

July 2013 was an amazing month for Manny. He celebrated his 21st birthday and he was selected to play in the All-Star Game.

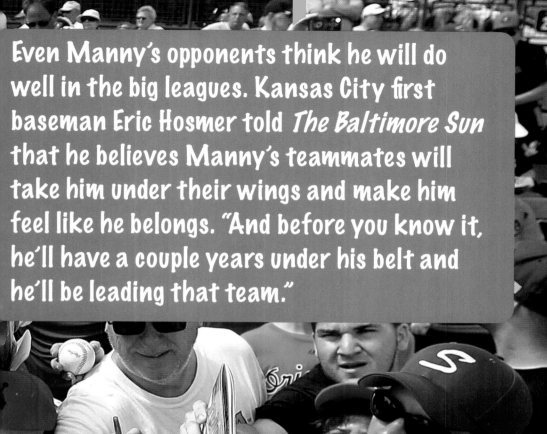

Even Manny's opponents think he will do well in the big leagues. Kansas City first baseman Eric Hosmer told *The Baltimore Sun* that he believes Manny's teammates will take him under their wings and make him feel like he belongs. "And before you know it, he'll have a couple years under his belt and he'll be leading that team."

FURTHER READING

Books

Gilbert, Sara. *World Series Champions: Baltimore Orioles.* Mankato, MN: Creative Paperbacks, 2013.

Rodriguez, Tania. *Superstars of Baseball: Alex Rodriguez.* Broomall, PA: Mason Crest, 2013.

Works Consulted

Connolly, Dan. "Orioles, Machado Agree to Terms." *The Baltimore Sun,* August 17, 2010.

Encina, Eduardo A. "Manny Ball." *The Baltimore Sun,* August 10, 2012.

Encina, Eduardo A. "Real Test is Yet to Come for Orioles' Manny Machado." *The Baltimore Sun,* August 13, 2012.

Knight, Molly. "Manny Machado's Big Night." *ESPN Magazine,* December 25, 2012. http://espn. go.com/mlb/story/_/ id/8766411/baltimore-orioles-3b-manny-machado-rose-stardom-sept-12-espn-magazine

White, Paul. "A-Rod, Admirer Go Head to Head." *USA Today,* October 8, 2012.

On the Internet

ESPN: Manny Machado http://espn.go.com/mlb/ player/_/id/31097/manny-machado

The Official Site of the Baltimore Orioles: Orioles Kids http://mlb.mlb.com/bal/ fan_forum/kids_index.jsp

INDEX

Baltimore Orioles   4, 6, 9, 11, 12, 15, 19, 21, 23, 25, 29

Brito, Geovany (uncle)   13

Brito Miami Private School   6

Camden Yards   12

childhood   9, 13, 15

curtain call   25

draft   4, 17

high school   6, 17

home runs   23

Hosmer, Eric   31

Jones, Adam   25, 28–29

Jordan, Joe   9

Kansas City Royals   21, 31

major league   11–15

Miami, Florida   6, 17

minor league teams   11, 15

New York Yankees   17

Nunez, Rosa (mother)   12

record   6, 23

Rodriguez, Alex (A-Rod)   17, 26–27

shortstop   4, 9, 11

third base   15, 17, 26